Rainbows, Angels and Unicorns!

D0995446

A child's first Spiritual book

By Eileen McCourt

Rainbows, Angels and Unicorns! A child's first Spiritual book

By Eileen McCourt

Rainbows, Angels and Unicorns! A child's first Spiritual book. This book was first published in Great Britain in paperback during April 2016.

The moral right of Eileen McCourt is to be identified as the author of this work and has been asserted by her in accordance with the Copyright, Designs and Patents Act of 1988.

ISBN-13: 978-1530635931

Copyright © April 2016 Eileen McCourt

Contents

ABOUT THE AUTHOR

Eileen McCourt is a graduate of University College Dublin with a Master's degree in History. She is a retired professional school teacher of History and English, and lives in Warrenpoint, County Down, Ireland.

A Reiki Grand Master, Eileen practises and teaches Reiki to all levels. She has also brought into this country, for the first time, many other healing modalities, from Spain and England, and practitioner and teacher courses for these are now available in Angel and Holistic centres around the country. A description of all these healing modalities is included in her book ' Working with Spirit: A World of Healing'.

This is Eileen's sixth book. It is written for young children, to give them an understanding, at an early age, of who they really are, why they are here and the meaning of life.

Her first book, 'Living the Magic', was published in December 2014.

Her second book, 'This Great Awakening', was published in September 2015.

Her third book, 'Spirit Calling: Are you Listening?' and her fourth book, ' Working with Spirit: A World of Healing', were both published in January 2016.

Her fifth book, ' Life's But a Game! Go With the Flow!' was published in February 2016. This is specifically aimed at teenagers and young adults, the majority of whom are under extreme pressure, and who feel greatly confused in today's world.

Eileen is currently working on her seventh book, which unveils the truth about the family of Jesus; the parts played by Mary Magdalene and Joseph of Arimathea in His life, and the Druid connection with Jesus and the early Christian Church.

Eileen has also recorded six meditation cds, accompanied by her brother, pianist Pat McCourt:

'Celestial Healing'

'Celestial Presence'

'Chakra Cleansing, Energising and Balancing'

'Ethereal Spirit'

'Open the Door to Archangel Michael'

'Healing with Archangel Raphael'

The list of outlets for books and cds, together with information on workshops and courses, for both practitioners and teachers, can be found on Eileen's website:

www.celestialhealing8.co.uk

e-mail: mccourteileen@yahoo.co.uk

ACKNOWLEDGEMENTS

I wish to express sincere thanks to the following, without whom this book would not have materialised:

My publishers, Don Hale OBE and Dr. Steve Green, for their tolerance and understanding!

Bronagh, Katie and Sarah at Mourne Office Supplies for their work and unfailing support;

My family and friends, both here on the Earth Plane and in the Higher Realms. In particular, Margaret Hurdman, who has just recently passed back to Spirit;

Shannon Hunter, for her illustrations. Shannon is a student of Art and Design at Southern Regional College, Newry, County Down. Her e-mail address is shanxox12@hotmail.com should you wish to contact her.

Thanks also to Dr. Steve Green for his input in the design of this book.

Michelle McLogan, for her input of exercises and experiments. Michelle works with primary school children and is involved in the Relax Kids Programme which teaches children how to deal with stress and anxiety. This programme is currently being incorporated into school and after-school activities in thirty seven countries around the world. Michelle's e-mail address is michellemclogan@yahoo.co.uk should you wish to contact her;

All those who buy my books and cds, and all who have attended my workshops and courses;

And last, but by no means least! Two beautiful little souls, who asked me not too long ago: "When are you going to write a book for us?"

Well, Orlaith and Lauren, here is that book! Hope you like it!

Finally, thank you Spirit for the gift of life, and for the blessings which you continue to shower upon us each and every day!

Eileen McCourt

17th March 2016

TO PARENTS AND GUARDIANS

Our most valuable, most priceless asset is our children.

Our children are the hope and salvation of our beloved Planet Earth.

On their young shoulders lies the responsibility to return our Planet to one of peace, harmony and love; to a world where all are treated equally; where all are respected and valued for the unique contribution each person makes; where everyone has sufficient and where everyone's needs are met in an abundant, supportive and loving Universe.

It's a big ask!

It is our responsibility to help our young people!

We need to help them by empowering them! We empower them by providing them with the knowledge that will enable and equip them to fulfil this great mission, this great challenge, that lies ahead of them.

Yes, knowledge is power! Truth is power!

And by empowering them, we are protecting them, we are freeing them from the contamination of gross materialism and greed so rampant in our world today.

The truth will set our young people free. Free from the shackles and chains of controlling religions and institutions which for over 2,000 years have dominated and dictated our lives, manipulating humanity for their own selfish, mercenary gains.

Our young people will live their lives in freedom and understanding that the answers to everything lie within each person. Their souls will soar and fly freely. Our young people will raise our world to new and enlightened heights for the betterment of all.

Our young people will take back their power!

Our young people will continue what we have begun. We have made the u-turn. We are on our way back to peace, love and harmony.

Our young people will fulfil their mission.

Armed with the truth, they cannot fail!

The truth always wins!

The future bodes well!

All is as it should be!

NAMASTE!

Eileen McCourt

17 March, 2016

TO ALL MY YOUNG READERS!

You are a very special person!

You are so special that this book has been written especially for you!

And in this book you will find out exactly why you are so special!

In this book, you will find out who you really are, and the wonderful powers you have to help everyone around you!

You will find exercises and experiments that will amaze you, and show you how lots of things really work in this world of ours.

And you will find out how, just because you cannot actually see something with your two eyes, then that does not mean that it does not exist!

For example, you cannot see the stars in the sky during the day. Nor can you see the sun in the sky during the night. But they are all still there! Likewise, when the boat sails over the horizon, it does not mean it has disappeared altogether. It just means you cannot see it any more. But it is still there!

Yes, there are lots of things all around us that we cannot always see with our two eyes! That's what helps to make this world of ours so exciting!

So come with me through the pages of this book and let's start to find out all about who you really are, and this beautiful world in which we all live!

But before we start, I invite you to meet Mattie and Maggie.

Hi I'm Mattie!

And I'm Maggie, and we want to be your friends!

Mattie and Maggie want to be your friends throughout this book.

I also invite you to colour in all the pictures, and in this way, you will make this book your very own! You will have created something very beautiful! Something very special just for you!

And remember! You are a special gift to the world!

Thank you for being you!

Have fun!

YOUR PHYSICAL BODY

Your physical body is just so amazing, so wonderful and so beautiful!

Your physical body is far more amazing than any computer could ever be! And a computer is certainly amazing!

But you can do much, much more than any computer can do!

Your physical body is what makes you able to run, jump, laugh, talk, eat, sleep, hear, see and do everything else that you do every day. No computer can do anything like what you can do!

Your physical body has a heart, a brain, a liver, lungs, kidneys, bones, veins and all the other organs that all work together to keep you healthy and alive. No computer has any of these!

Computers can only do what someone else programmes them to do. You do not need anyone to programme your physical body for you! Your own amazing brain is constantly sending messages all around your body, telling it what you want it to do.

No computer has a brain like yours! In fact no computer has got any sort of brain at all!

And your physical body can experience all sorts of feelings. That includes all the highs and all the lows, all the fun, all the laughter, all the happiness. A computer most certainly cannot do that! A computer cannot feel anything! That's because it is really just a lump of metal all wired up, being worked by someone else. A bit like a puppet on a string! It cannot think, it cannot laugh, it cannot do anything for itself unless someone programmes it to do so. Yes, a computer is a great machine, but that is all it is! A machine!

You are much more than just a machine!

What an amazing body you have!

YOUR FIVE PHYSICAL SENSES

You are able to experience life through your five physical senses.

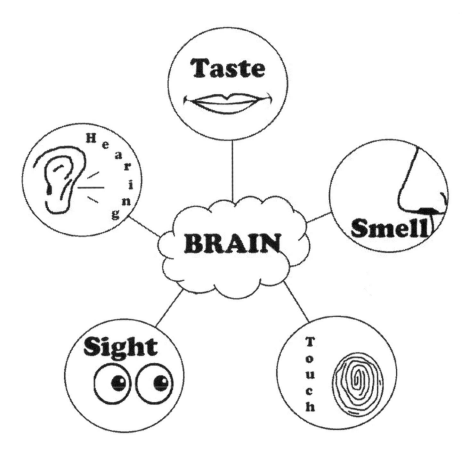

First, you can see all that is in front of you and around you with your eyes. All the people, the places, the animals, the colours of the flowers, the sky, the moon and the stars.

5

How wonderful is that!

Secondly, you can hear all the sounds around you with your ears. The birds singing, twittering and tweeting; the wind sighing in the trees; the leaves rustling on the ground in autumn; the rivers and streams gurgling as the water tumbles down over the stones; people laughing and talking; thunder roaring across the sky; your dog barking and your cat mewing.

How wonderful is that!

Thirdly, you can smell all the different scents in the air around you. The perfume from the flowers and trees; the refreshing scent in the air after a shower of rain; the fragrance after the grass has been cut; the tempting aroma of the dinner in the oven; the comforting scent from your pet; the sweet, earthy scent of your baby brother or sister just after their bath.

How wonderful is that!

Fourthly, you can taste everything with your tongue and your mouth. All the different flavours in your food; the salt water when you are in the sea; you can even taste the rain when it falls on your face!

How wonderful is that!

Lastly, you can feel through touching. The softness of your clothes; the lovely furry coat of your pet; the velvety feel of the grass or the gritty feel of the sand when you walk in your bare feet; the warmth of the soil in your hands; the wind blowing softly against your cheeks; the coolness of the rain on your skin; the warmth of the sun on your body.

How wonderful is that!

What an amazing body you have!

And because it is so amazing, you need to look after it!

You need to eat the proper food to keep your body healthy. You need to get sufficient sleep so that your body will have enough energy to do what you want it to do. You need to exercise your body to help it to grow strong so that it will be able to carry you around.

Love your physical body!

The more you love and care for your body, the longer it will be able to keep you alive. You might even live to be over one hundred years old!

How amazing is that!

YOUR OTHER BODY

You have just seen how wonderful your physical body is and all the amazing things you can do with this amazing, wonderful body of yours.

However, you have another body besides your amazing physical body!

Yes! You actually have two bodies!

This other body is called your Spiritual body, or your soul.

So what is the difference between these two bodies? And why do you need two bodies anyway? Is one body not enough?

You need two bodies, because together they make up the whole you! They work together to make sure you are living a happy, contented life, full of fun and laughter.

Your physical body is only temporary. That means it is only meant to stay with you during this life-time. Just like an old coat, when you no longer need it, you put is aside. So too, there will come a time when you no longer need your physical body. And just like that old coat, you will now cast off your physical body. You will not need it any longer!

But your Spiritual body? Now that's a very different matter!

Your Spiritual body, you see, is not like your physical body. Your physical body is meant for this life-time only and it will someday wear out, and then you will have no more need for it. But your Spiritual body, your soul, is immortal. That means that it will go on forever and ever. It will never ever wear out.

WOW! Isn't that so amazing? That you have a body that will go on forever and ever!

So, if your physical body is not going to last forever, while your Spiritual body will always go on forever, which of these two bodies do you think is the most important?

Your physical body? Is that most important?

Or your Spiritual body? Is that most important?

So how else do these two bodies of yours differ?

While your physical body is the body that everyone can see, your Spiritual body is the body that cannot be seen. That's why we call them different names. Your physical body is called your physical body because it is physically visible, while on the other hand, your Spiritual body is called your Spiritual body because it is invisible.

This Spiritual body of yours is deep inside your physical body, and it is this body that connects you to God. Your Spiritual body, also called your soul, cannot be seen by anyone. Even a surgeon, when operating on someone, does not see a soul floating about inside that person's body! Most definitely not!

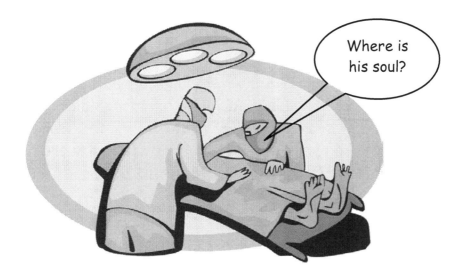

Now, remember you read about how you need to keep your physical body healthy? Well, you also need to keep your Spiritual body healthy too.

And how do you keep your Spiritual body healthy?

You keep your Spiritual body healthy by keeping your soul happy! That's because, remember, your soul is your Spiritual body!

And the big question is, how do you keep your soul happy?

It really is very easy to keep your soul happy!

All you have to do to keep your soul happy is, continue to do what you like doing and what you enjoy doing. That's all! How easy is that?

If you like painting, then your soul is really happy when you are painting. If you like music, dancing, singing, writing, playing sport, making things, baking, pottering about in the garden, messing about in boats, or riding your pony, then your soul enjoys all of that too. In other words, when you are enjoying yourself and having fun, then your soul just loves it! You are making your soul so happy!

You make your soul happy too, by being kind to other people, by sharing what you have with them, especially with those who do not have as much as you have.

Who do you share with?

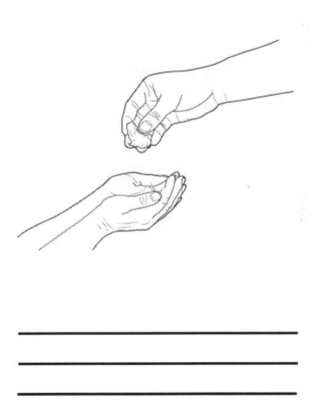

_____

_____

_____

Your soul really loves it when you are kind to animals; when you say good things about other people; when you refuse to carry gossip or stories about other people; when you refuse to join in with others who laugh or scoff at other people and when you defend others against bullies, or those who are causing them hurt in any way.

So, you can now see how both of your amazing bodies need to be cared for and looked after. And the more you care for the both of them, then the happier you will be! That's because your two bodies go together, and work together to look after you and make you the person you are!

YOUR THIRD EYE

Right in the middle of your forehead you have something very special and very amazing!

This is your 'Third Eye'.

Remember how you learned about your two bodies? Your physical body and your Spiritual body, also called your soul? And your five physical senses?

Well, this Third Eye of yours belongs to your Spiritual body. Your Spiritual body has some senses too, just as your physical body has, and your Third Eye is one of these Spiritual senses. And because it is a Spiritual sense, that's the reason why you cannot see it. And because it is a Spiritual sense, it is very, very powerful!

But you can feel it sometimes! You can sense with it!

You can sense with it when you sit very quietly, by yourself, away from all the noise and chatter.

It is through your Third Eye that God sends you messages. It is through your Third Eye that you just know something without being told about it. But you need to be sitting very quietly in order to see these messages.

When you sit very quietly and think about your Third Eye, you are doing what is called *'meditating'*.

'Meditation' is a Spiritual exercise and is very good for your soul, in just the same way as physical exercise is very good for your physical body. When you meditate, your soul connects with God in a very special way, and God can get messages through to you much more easily when you are not being distracted by all the things going on around you.

Your Third Eye is also very amazing because there is a great beam of White Light that you can send out through your Third Eye to help anyone who needs help. Maybe you have a sore foot? You can imagine a great beam of White Light coming out of your Third Eye and being directed at your sore foot, sending it healing. You won't see the White Light of course, because it is a Spiritual Light, and therefore not visible to the human eye.

As you grow older and learn more about your Spiritual body, which is your soul, you will become much more aware of your Third Eye and you will learn how to open it in order to sense when you are seeing things through it.

Yes, your Third Eye is an amazing sense in your Spiritual body!

THE REAL YOU

Now you know that there is more to you than just your physical body! Much more!

You are a body AND a soul!

BUT! Where has your soul come from?

Your soul has come from God.

God is a beautiful, shining, shimmering White Light, filled with unending love for all of us, and for all the other forms of life that share this Planet Earth with us.

One day, God decided He wanted to create lots of life for Himself to enjoy, so He sent out lots and lots of shining, shimmering sparks from His great bright White Light.

These sparks are therefore parts of God. And guess what these sparks of God are called?

These beautiful, shining sparks of God are called *'Souls'*.

And guess who is one of these precious souls!

Yes! YOU are!

So, if you are a soul, a spark of God, and God is a great shimmering White Light, then what does that make you?

That means that you too are a great shimmering White Light, because you are made from God!

You carry that great White Light around inside you all the time, because, remember, that great White Light is your soul. And your soul and your body work together to make you the beautiful, kind, loving person you really are!

Your body is really a means, a vehicle, a form of transport, if you like, to carry your soul around for this life-time. It is like a house that your God Light lives in while you are here on Earth.

So now you know who the REAL YOU is!

The REAL YOU is that beautiful, shining, shimmering spark of God Light living inside you, in your precious soul.

WOW!

And now you can see why you must take care of both your body AND your soul! And you now know how to do all that! Just be happy, laugh a lot, have lots of fun, and your precious soul will be so happy and so healthy!

Now, if your soul is so precious, as it is, because it has come from the great God Light, and because it is a part of God, then every other soul is the same. All souls have come from God, so all souls are white, shimmering Light inside all the other bodies around us.

So, you must love and be kind to all other people! And you can now see why!

You must be kind and helpful to other people because they too, are a part of this great God White Light, and you must try and see this beautiful Light shining out from them.

And because you now see everyone as a part of God, just like you, with God's Light inside them, then you will not criticise anyone or think badly of them, or treat them unkindly or unfairly.

WOW!

If we could all remember that each and every person on this Earth is a spark of God's great shimmering Light, then there would be no wars or fighting! What a wonderful world this would be!

And you can start right here and now to make this world a wonderful world, simply by seeing everyone you meet and everyone you know as the bright, shimmering God Light they really are!

See how powerful you really are! See how powerful you are as a part of God's shimmering, radiant, beautiful White Light!

UNDERSTANDING ENERGY

Before we go any further, we need to understand what the word *'Energy'* means and we need to understand how energy works.

Everything is energy. Absolutely everything!

And that includes all of us!

And the thing about energy is that it never dies or ends. It just changes form.

So, because we are energy, we never die. We just change our energy form.

There are countless forms of energy, all operating on what we call 'different energy vibration levels', from the very highest level right down to the very lowest level. And we are surrounded by all these different levels of energy all the time. We cannot see them, of course, because they are Spiritual energy.

It's just like the television in your house. When you are tuned into one particular channel, where are all the other channels? Away off somewhere else?

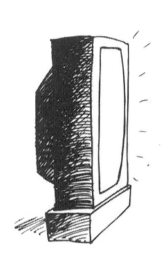

Hardly!

All the other channels are still around you, but on different frequency levels. And you cannot see any of these other channels, only the one channel you are tuned into. Even when your television is not turned on, all these different frequencies are still in your house, but because you are not tuned in, you cannot see them.

Get the message?

And that's just what the energy around us is like!

We cannot see all the different levels, because we are not tuned into them!

So all energy vibrates at a different level. Right?

So all of us are vibrating at different levels. Right?

And the closer to God we are, and the more we know about, and are aware of, our Spiritual body, and the more we care for our Spiritual body, then the higher our energy vibration is.

And the higher our energy vibration is, then the easier it is for us to tune into other energy vibration levels that are all around us.

The angels and saints are all very close to God, so their energy vibration is on a very high level indeed!

Remember you learned earlier about how God created all the souls from the great White Light?

Well, all those souls were a part of God, so they were on a really high vibrational level, in Heaven.

Then, when you decided you wanted to come and live on Planet Earth for a while, you changed your energy to a lower level, in order to be able to fit in here. Your new energy took the form of a physical body.

Just before you were born, your soul left Heaven and entered into your physical body. Your soul, however, felt that very difficult, changing from such a high energy vibration in Heaven to this much slower vibrational energy here on Planet Earth. So, as a little baby, you slept a lot of the time.

That was because your soul needed time to get used to this Planet Earth energy. Then, as you grew older, your soul became more comfortable in your physical body, and you did not sleep as much.

So you see, we need to understand all about energy, how energy works and how it affects us all.

Everything we do sends out an energy vibration into space. So too, every word we speak. Even our thoughts send out energy vibrations.

And whatever kind of energy we send out always attracts the same kind of energy back to us. Fact!

So we must always be careful about the kind of energy we send out in our actions, words and thoughts.

Perhaps you remember some time in your life trying to get off school by telling your mummy you had a pain in your tummy, or you had a sore head? And, indeed, you probably thought you had got away with it if you were allowed to stay off school? But I bet you, that before that day was out, you really did have a sore head or a sick tummy! Right?

See what happened here? You sent out the energy through your thoughts and words that you had a sore head or a sick tummy, and that energy drew the same thing back to you! So you ended up with a sore head or a sick tummy!

That's the way energy works!

Think of energy like a boomerang. You know that a boomerang is made in such a way that it always comes back to you? Well, that's exactly the way energy works!

So you need to be very careful about the kind of energy you are sending out. And why do you need to be careful? Because it will all boomerang back to you again!

So if we send out thoughts or words of anger, envy, spite, hatred or unkindness in any form, then watch out! It's that boomerang again! It's always that boomerang!

OUCH! THAT HURT!

On the other hand, when you send out kind, loving, caring words and thoughts, those kind, loving, caring words and thoughts will come back to you again in a really loving energy form.

Only this time, the boomerang will be different. You don't need to duck to avoid this boomerang! You can catch it!

So always think carefully before you speak about anyone! Once you send out that energy, you cannot delete it or call it back and replace it! And you have to live with the good or the harm you have caused to happen!

Now think about this! When you leave for school in the morning, how do you feel? Grumpy? Cross face? Bad mood?

Remember! Your feelings and thoughts send out energy from you! So if you are heading off to school with a big scowl on your face, then you know what is going to happen!

Here comes that boomerang!

Here come all the other cross faces, scowls, and bad moods you have attracted back to yourself!

What a miserable day this is turning out to be!

On the other hand, if you are heading off to school full of happiness and enthusiasm, with a lovely smiley face, then you know that you are going to have a wonderful, exciting day. And why? Because you are sending out the energy that will attract all sorts of exciting, amazing, loving things and people back to you!

And the good news is, that if you start off your day with a cross face and a scowl, you are not doomed to cross faces and scowls for the rest of the day!

And why not? Because you can change your thoughts any time you want! You can change your thoughts, and when you change your thoughts, you change the energy you are sending out! And you know what that means!

Yes! You are in control! You are in control of the energy you are sending out, and therefore, you are in control of the type of energy that comes back to you! It's as simple as that!

And that explains why you have certain friends! Your friends are your friends because you have drawn them into your life with the particular energy you have been sending out.

BUT! The thing about energy is that it is changing all the time.

When your energy changes, as it does, because your feelings and moods change all the time, you now send out your new energy. And this new energy you are now sending out might not be the same as the energy of your friends.

That's because we all change our energy at different rates and different times. So you see, this explains why you might lose some of your friends from time to time. And this new energy you are sending out now draws new friends to you!

And this is all good news, because it means that you will always have friends who match your own energy! Get the picture?

Very often, yes, it hurts when some of your friends stop being your friends. You might wonder what you have done to upset them. But you have done nothing wrong! Do not be angry with them or feel spiteful towards them. Because remember! You now know what that will get you! A sharp slap from an angry boomerang!

So instead of being angry and cross with them, thank them for all the lessons you learned from them, and send them love. And just see what you get back!

Perhaps your mummy and daddy are separated and do not live together any more? Perhaps you are living with one of your parents and you get to see your other parent as often as you like? Or perhaps you do not see your other parent any more at all?

Well, let's look at what is happening here!

It's all about energy again! It's always about energy! And how energy is always changing!

When your parents met and fell in love, that was because their energies were similar, so they were attracted to each other. Then you arrived!

But you now know that energy never stays the same. Sometimes when two people love each other, they grow and change together, so their energies continue to match. And that is wonderful! But very often, one person's energy changes faster than the other person's energy, and then they begin to drift apart, because their energies no longer match as well as they did before. That's when the harsh and unkind words start, and the home is not as happy as before.

Well, now you know what is happening!

And now you know that if your parents have split up, it's because their energies no longer match. That's all! It happens all the time! And why? Because energy is always changing! And we are always sending out energy in our actions, in our words and in our thoughts! That's why!

It's all got to do with that changing energy! Like everything else in life! But the good news is that you yourself are in control of the energy you are sending out! The energy you are sending out attracts similar energy back to you.

So, if you are not having a good day, you know what to do!

Change your thoughts! And then your energy will change! So will your day!

You are in control!

WOW!

EXPERIMENT!

You now know how energy works!

And you know you can control energy through your thoughts!

Well, just to prove it, try this experiment!

Cut an apple in half and place each half in the same kind of container, side by side.

Label one half 'BAD APPLE' and the other half 'LOVELY APPLE'.

 **Lovely Apple**

 Bad Apple

You can place some stickers above each.

On the stickers for the BAD APPLE, write down what or who makes you angry or what makes you feel sad.

On the stickers for the LOVELY APPLE, write down what or who makes you feel happy and write down some things you like.

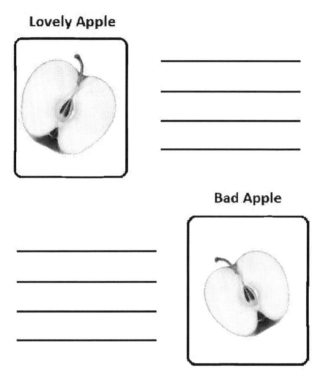

Lovely Apple

_____

_____

_____

_____

Bad Apple

_____

_____

_____

_____

Now, all you have to do is, every time you think of any of these words you have written, direct your feelings into the relevant half of the apple.

Over the next few days, just watch what happens!

YOUR AURA

You now know that every living thing is filled with energy.

And that includes you!

Your physical body is surrounded on all sides by an energy field. This energy field is called your **'Aura'**.

The energy in your aura is like electricity. It is called *'electro-magnetic energy'* and it surrounds your entire body, radiating outwards. If you did not have this aura, then you would not exist.

Everyone has an aura around their physical body. So too does every other form of life, for example trees, flowers, animals, mountains and rivers.

Your energy goes out through your aura in vibrations. You read about vibrations and energy in the last chapter. Remember?

Animals sense your energy vibration very quickly. A dog can tell if you are scared because of the frightened and nervous vibrations you are sending out through your aura. So can a horse. A horse knows if you are nervous when you are riding it, because it senses your fear.

So, you see, your aura tells a lot about you!

First of all, your aura shows how healthy your body is. If you are feeling really great and in a good mood, having lots of fun, then your aura will show up as very bright all around you. On the other hand, if you are feeling ill or in a bad mood, then your aura will not be so bright. So your aura acts as a sort of barometer, showing what condition your body is in.

Your aura also shows how happy your soul is. Again, if your soul is really happy, and is learning a lot of lessons, then your aura will be really bright. On the other hand, If your soul is not happy, then this too will show up in your aura, only this time your aura will not be so bright.

Some people can see auras very clearly. Perhaps you can see the aura around your pet? Around the trees? Around the flowers?

You can get a photograph taken of your aura. This is taken with a special camera and is called 'Kirlian Photography'. The man who invented it was called Semyon Kirlian, so this photography is called after him.

So you have this energy field all around your body.

And you know all about energy and how it works! You know that when it goes out from you, it attracts the same kind of energy back.

If you are angry, then your vibration going out through your aura will make other people uncomfortable, and they will not want to be near you.

On the other hand, if you are sending out bright energy because you have a smiley face and you are in a good mood, then you will attract more smiley, happy faces back to you. You will have a great day!

However, something else happens when you send out bright, happy energy!

Unfortunately, when you send out bright happy energy through your aura, you do not just attract other bright, happy auras! You also attract the not-so-bright auras! Other people who are not happy and do not have a bright aura around them, see your bright light and want to get to it to take some of your happy bright energy for themselves. We call these people *'Energy Vampires'*.

Energy vampires come in all shapes and sizes. Energy vampires do exactly what it says on the tin. They suck at your lovely bright energy, and this can leave you very tired, even totally exhausted sometimes.

So who or what are these energy vampires? And how do you recognise them?

Energy vampires are those people who criticise you, or say horrible things about you, or who put you down in any way.

Energy vampires are those people who are jealous of you and tell lies about you. Energy vampires are those people who bully you or treat you unfairly.

But energy vampires are just not always people!

Your computer is an energy vampire! Your mobile phone is an energy vampire! The micro-wave in your kitchen is an energy vampire! And yes! Your television is an energy vampire!

That's because all of these send out negative electro-energy rays into the air, and this affects your energy.

BUT! The good news is that you can protect yourself against all these energy vampires!

You can protect your own beautiful, pure, clean energy!

You can protect your beautiful clean aura so that no energy vampire can get anywhere near it!

PROTECTING YOUR AURA

You can protect your aura and your energy very easily!

There is a very exciting and very amazing method you can use, and it never fails!

All you have to do to protect yourself is to imagine, in your mind, a great big circle of White Light surrounding your entire body.

This White Light is the White Light of God, and it will always protect you.

Remember reading about this White Light before? When you were learning about how God created you from His own great White Light?

Well, this is the same God Light that is now going to protect you.

This God Light will also protect other people for you as well. You might want to protect your parents, your brothers and sisters, your friends or your pets.

Well, you can do this! All you have to do is, in your mind, draw the White Light around them, and then you will know they will be safe from any harm.

You can also protect your house, your car, your bicycle, by putting them all inside the White Light.

The White Light will also protect you when you are scared, for example, in a thunderstorm, or in any other situation where you are afraid. Even in your dreams!

So you see, you need never be afraid! And why not? Because you always have the White Light to protect you!

Always!

HEALING HANDS

Let's go back to what you learned at the beginning of this book about your two bodies.

Remember learning about your five physical senses that go with your amazing physical body?

Remember, too, learning about your Spiritual body, also called your soul, and how that has senses as well?

Remember your Third Eye? That is one of the senses in your Spiritual body.

But you also have other senses in your Spiritual body!

You have very powerful senses in the palms of your hands!

And you can use these hand senses to bring healing to yourself, to your friends and to your pets.

Isn't that just amazing?

Let's see how it all works! First of all, let me remind you of the most famous person in history. Do you know who that might be?

The most famous person in history is, of course, Jesus.

When Jesus was living here on Earth over 2,000 years ago, He healed a lot of people.

Now remember what you learned about energy and energy vibrations? And how we all send out different energy vibrations through our aura?

Remember too, how you learned that the closer to God you are, then the higher and more powerful the energy you send out?

Well, Jesus came to this Earth from a very, very high energy vibrational level. That's why He was able to perform all sorts of miracles and heal so many people!

But what was Jesus actually doing when he was healing people? Remember reading about how your aura shows how you are feeling? If your aura is bright, you are feeling well, and if your auras is not so bright you are not feeling very well. So when Jesus was healing what was he doing?

Jesus was moving energy around! Jesus was moving blocked energy from people's aura and making their aura strong and healthy again!

WOW!

Now, believe it or not, we all have energy flowing through the palms of our hands, and we can all use that energy to help heal people.

We can't, of course, heal as well as Jesus was able to heal, and you know why! Because our energy is nowhere nearly as high as the energy of Jesus was.

But lots of people have been trained to work with this energy. We call these people **'Holistic Healers'**. Perhaps you have heard of the word **'Reiki'**?

Reiki is a way of moving energy in order to heal people. Maybe your mum or dad is a Reiki healer?

The healing energy comes out of the palms of the healer's hands, so that is why it is also called **'hands-on healing'**. Sometimes the energy is hot, sometimes cooler. But it is always good! And sometimes it might not cure the physical pain or illness, but it always brings emotional and mental healing. The person always feels so much better afterwards!

When you get older, you might like to work with the different energies in order to heal people.

WOW!

EXERCISE!

The word 'CHI' is a Japanese word meaning 'ENERGY'.

Lots of sports people understand this word and there are many sports where this energy is used by moving it around.

One of these sports is called 'TAEKWONDO'.

Another is 'KARATE'.

There are also people who practise meditation and relaxation using energy, by moving it about.

One of these is 'YOGA'. Have you heard of YOGA?

Another is 'TAI-CHI'.

Have you heard of 'ACUPUNCTURE'?

ACUPUNTURE is where very fine needles are placed along the energy centres in the body, in order to make the energy move around the body better, helping to heal the body.

So you see, it is very important to understand all about energy!

Can you think of any other people who move energy around in their work? You have just read about them in the last chapter!

WHERE HAVE I COME FROM?

Now you know all about your two bodies! You know about your physical body and you know about your Spiritual body, which is called your soul.

You know where your soul has come from. You know your soul is a spark of God Light, very bright, very beautiful.

So, let's now go back to your physical body again. Where has it come from?

Well, you know that you were born into this life from your mum's tummy.

But remember! Your beautiful soul is a spark of God Light. That means your soul came from God. So your soul came from God into your mum's tummy.

Before you were born, you were with God in Heaven. Then one day, you decided you would like to live on Earth for a while. Then you looked really closely at the people on Earth and you decided who you would like to have as your mum and dad.

Yes! We all get to choose our own parents! How cool is that?

While you were waiting for your mum to have her new baby, you spent a lot of time being near her, looking after her, making sure she was fine.

Then, when it came near the time for her baby to be born, your soul gently moved into that new baby. Your soul joined with that little body in your mum's tummy. You became that little baby!

And then you were born!

You were born with two bodies!

Your beautiful physical body and your beautiful shining, shimmering Spiritual body, your soul.

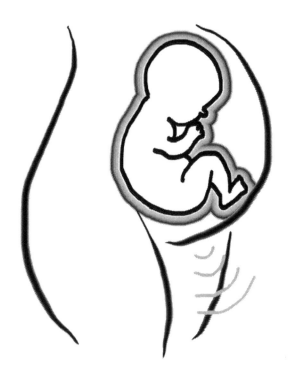

WHY AM I HERE?

As you have just seen, you are here because you want to be here! Nobody forced you to come and live on Earth. You chose to come here yourself, and you also chose your own parents to help you to live here.

Why am I here?

And why did you decide to come and live here on Planet Earth?

You decided to come and live here on Planet Earth because your beautiful soul wanted to learn some lessons, and the more lessons it can learn, then the closer to God it, and therefore you, will be.

In actual fact, this is most probably not the first time you have lived here on Planet Earth! You have probably been here many times before, and you will probably be here many more times. That's because your soul really wants to be as close to God as possible, and so it wants to learn as many lessons as possible in order to get closer to God in Heaven.

Think about how everything in Nature goes to sleep for the winter. Then, when spring comes, all the flowers and trees waken up again full of life after their refreshing long rest. We call this long winter sleep Nature's *'hibernation'*.

Just like everything in Nature, like all the trees, all the flowers, some of the little animals, you too go for a long sleep or a long rest after each of your life-times. We call this **'Reincarnation'**.

This means that after each life-time, you go back to Heaven for a while in order to rest. Then, when you decide you want to return to Planet Earth again, you start to look around to see who you will choose as your parents this time.

It's just like a great big merry-go-round!

You get on, then you get off, then you get back on again to have another go, another ride on the carousel. And all the time you are having fun! And each time you get on, you can choose which ride you want to go on!

That's just like life!

And in just the same way as you can choose which ride you go for on the merry-go-round, so too, you can choose everything for your next go on the **merry-go-round of life!**

How awesome is that?

Cool or what?

I CAN CHOOSE!

So, you have just learned that you get to choose your own parents.

But that's not the only choice you have on the merry-go-round of life! Far from it!

Apart from you yourself deciding whether or not you want to come to Planet Earth, deciding when you will come, and deciding who will be your parents, you get to choose much, much more!

Once you have made the decision to come back again on the merry-go-round of life, you have a lot of thinking to do and a lot of plans to make!

Everything has to be just right for your next life-time! Nothing can be left to chance or just luck!

Each of your life-times is planned by you with great care.

And where are you when you are planning all this?

You are in Heaven with God. That's where you go back to after every life-time. Remember what you learned about 'reincarnation'? How you go back to Heaven for a while after each of your lives here on Earth? And when you are in Heaven, you are planning your next life, your next set of adventures! And you get to choose all those next adventures! And your friends are helping you! They might even choose to play a part in your life!

How exciting!

So, you, and you only, will decide who you are going to be. Where are you going to live? What kind of a physical body will you have this time to carry your soul around?

Yes, you will design your own body!

Cool!

But the most important thing you have got to decide is what lessons you are coming here to Planet Earth to learn.

And why is that the most important decision?

Well, apart from that being the main reason why you are returning again anyway, those lessons you want to learn will determine who you will be, where you will live, what work you will do and what kind of life you will live.

So you see, everything in your life depends on the lessons you yourself choose to learn! That's how important those lessons are!

And just to put some fun into it all, there are lots of hidden clues you need to find about learning those lessons!

WHO OR WHAT IS GOD?

Remember reading about where you have come from? How you were created by God from the great God Light? How God sent out millions and millions of sparks from the great White Light, and these sparks were called souls? And how you are one of these beautiful precious souls?

Well, now consider this!

You have learned how everything is energy. You have learned that you are energy. And you have learned that energy is always changing form. Right?

So, if you are energy, and you were created by God out of the great White God Light, then that must mean that the great White God Light is also energy!

Yes! God is energy! And in that huge massive energy that is God, is included everything and everybody that ever has been, and ever will be! That huge great White Light of energy covers absolutely everything!

So God is actually everything and everybody!

Picture a huge white light, bursting with energy and spreading out to cover absolutely everything and everyone throughout the entire Earth, throughout all the other universes and planets and throughout space.

WOW! That's some light! That's some energy!

And this energy is what we call God. This energy is what we call the great *'Universal Consciousness of God'*.

That means that nothing, absolutely nothing, can exist outside of this great energy that we call God. It is from this massive energy called God that all life comes.

Let me make this easier for you to understand!

Think of all the electrical appliances in your house. You have a cooker, a fridge, a micro-wave, a washing machine, a dishwasher, a television, lights and a computer. And these are only some of all the electrical gadgets you can see around your house!

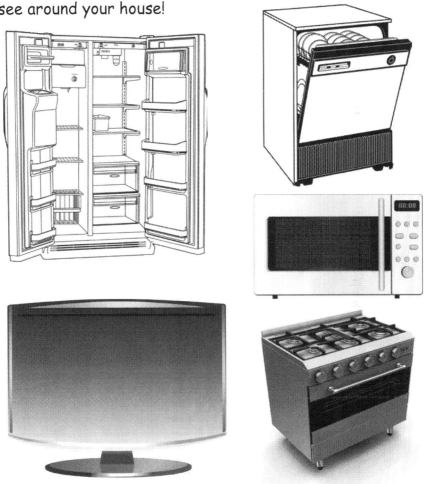

Now you know that these all have to be switched on before they will work. Right?

Switched onto what?

Switched onto the electricity main supply, the electricity main network! And then and only then will they be able to work!

And in just the same way as that electricity energy that powers your electrical gadgets in your house comes from the main electricity grid, so too, God is the energy supply that creates everything and everybody.

Get the message?

Now here's another way to help you to understand God!

Think of the huge ocean.

Think of all the life in the ocean.

Think of all the marine life. All the fish, all the big mammals, all the vegetation, all the algae, and even all the waves! All of this is only in existence because the ocean is in existence. Right?

If the ocean was not there, then none of any of these forms of life would be there!

And why not?

Because the ocean has given life to all of these!

Now, think of the waves.

The waves start as little ripples, build up to a crest and then crash. When they crash, where do they go? They go back down into the ocean again, getting ready to build up into another wave again. See how their energy is just changing form?

If the wave could speak, then, when it is a wave, it would shout out: "Hey, man! Look at me! I'm a wave!"

Then, when it falls back into the ocean it would shout: "Hey you guys! Look at me! I'm the ocean!"

So, you see, we are all part of the great God Energy, and we cannot exist outside of this great God Energy. Just as you have seen how the ocean contains all the life in the ocean, and that life is only there because the ocean is there!

Understand?

WE ARE ALL ONE

Now you know that God is a huge big mass of energy that includes absolutely everything and everybody. And nothing can exist outside of God.

So, if we are all in the God Energy, and are all part of God, then that must mean that we are all One. Right?

Perhaps you have learned in school about some of the teachings of Jesus?

About when he told his disciples: *"If you do it to one of these, my least brethren, you do it to me."*

What Jesus meant here was that whatever we do to anyone else, we also do that to ourselves, because we are all One in the great God Energy.

That means that we must be kind to everyone, we must not hurt anyone, we must not be cruel to anyone!

And why not?

Simply because we are all One! I am you and you are me! We are all made from, and share in, the same God Energy.

And why would I want to hurt you? That means I am hurting myself! How stupid would that be?

So you see, we all need to care for, and look after, each other!

And why? Because we are all One! That's why!

WHAT IS LOVE ?

Love, Love, Love!

Love is all around us! *Love* is in the air!

Love is what makes the world go around!

You have come here to Planet Earth to spread *love.*

We tell people we love them! We tell our pets we love them!

We love ice-cream. We love going to the cinema. We love going away on holidays. We love Christmas. We love the long summer days. We love shopping. We love football. We love just hanging out with our friends.

We certainly seem to do a whole lot of loving! As the song goes: *"There's a whole lot of loving going on in the world!"*

So what do you think love actually means?

Do you love your parents in the same way you love ice-cream? Hardly! The same way you love your football? I don't think so!

So how does the way in which you love ice-cream differ from the love you have for your parents or for your friends?

Well, first of all, you give your parents and your friends lots of hugs and kisses. Right?

This is you showing them you *love* them. Right?

Would you be very surprised if I told you that most people do not understand what *love* really means?

Because *love* does not just mean giving hugs and kisses!

Love means a lot more than just hugs and kisses!

Let me explain!

Remember you read about how all of us are made from the great God Light? How each of us is a spark of God Light?

Remember how I explained that we have all got to look for that beautiful Light inside everybody?

Remember how I explained what would happen if we could just see this beautiful Light inside everyone? How this would be a wonderful world?

And remember reading about the real you? How the real you and the real everyone else is this beautiful Light inside us all?

Well, the real meaning of love is that we see each other as this beautiful Light. And because we see each other as this beautiful, shining Light, this God Light, then we do not criticise anyone, we do not judge anyone, we do not treat anyone unkindly. And why not? Simply because we recognise everyone as a spark of God Light. And we send them only *unconditional love.*

And what exactly is unconditional love?

Unconditional love means that there are no conditions attached. Unconditional love means that we do not say to anyone: *"I will love you if you buy me..........."* or " *I will love you if you take me........".*

Every time you use the words *"if"* or *"on condition that....."*, when you are telling someone that you love them, then that is not love at all! That is you trying to control or manipulate someone!

When you try to control or manipulate someone, then that is not good. That is you being a bully, trying to force them into doing what you want them to do by using love as a bribe, or threatening to not love them if they do not do as you want.

Think of your pet. Your pet never criticises you or looks as if he is disgusted with you, no matter what you have done or how untidy you look! That's because your pet has unconditional love for you, and sees you always as the bright God Light you really are. You are always perfect in your pet's eyes, just the way you are.

So that is what unconditional love means! It means seeing every other person, and seeing yourself too, of course, as the perfect bright shining Light each of us really is. And then when we see them as perfect, we do not judge or criticise them. We accept them exactly as they are and we see only the good in them. That is us really loving them!

And love never asks for anything in return. You don't give a birthday present to all your friends in the hope that when your birthday comes around, you will get loads of presents in return.

Or do you?

Well, if you do, then you need to remember the boomerang! If those are the thoughts you are sending out, you know what's on its way back to you!

OUCH! THAT REALLY HURT!

Of course it did, and you know where it came from! You were in control! And look what happened!

So now you know what love really means. And yes, keep giving your hugs and kisses to all those people you love.

Hugs and kisses are good because they make people feel happy. But remember the real meaning of love!

And remember that everyone needs love. The world needs love. And you have lots of love to give to everyone! And of course, the more unconditional love you give out, the more love you get back in return!

Everyone's a winner!

COLLECTING BROWNIE POINTS

Remember why you have come to live on Planet Earth?

You have come to learn some lessons in order for your soul to get closer to God in Heaven.

And you yourself have chosen which lessons to learn.

And the most important lesson of all to learn is to show love to other people and to all forms of life.

And you have also learned what love really means!

So, as you are learning all these lessons, you are collecting brownie points every time you learn something.

And the more brownie points you collect, then you know what happens! The closer you will be to God when you return to Heaven after this life-time!

So you need to collect as many brownie points as you can! You cannot afford to miss any chance of collecting brownie points! So you have got to keep your eyes and ears open all the time to spot how you can earn another brownie point!

Brownie points are so precious, and in order to find the hidden clues as to how you can earn them, you need to know where to look!

When you find the hidden clues, they will guide you to see how you can earn brownie points, and the more brownie points you earn, the happier your soul will be, and then the closer to God you will be in Heaven!

So you see, life's just like a game! A game of fun! And you are going to play this game of fun!

FINDING THE HIDDEN CLUES!

So, you now know that life is just a game! A game of fun!

A game of finding the hidden clues and putting them all together!

The clues that will help you to learn the lessons you need to learn!

And every lesson you learn gets you more brownie points!

And you know what more brownie points mean!

More brownie points mean getting closer to God!

So, let's get started! Let's play the game!

First of all, we need to know where to look in order to find these hidden clues.

Now, say, for example, you have decided to learn to be more charitable and kind.

You are not going to learn that from your school books! There are no clues in there!

No!

You will find the clues for this piece of the puzzle in the poor people all around the world. They are the ones who are offering you the chance to be more charitable and kind, and to share what you have with all those people who have very little.

The poor homeless person you pass on the street! There's your first clue! There's your first move towards getting more brownie points! You can't afford to miss!

Now let's see where else we can look to find these clues!

What about when your mummy is really busy and very tired? There's another clue!

You can help her! You can ask her what little jobs you can do for her. Maybe you could just tidy your room, or put the rubbish in the bin, or help her with the washing-up. More brownie points!

You're doing just great!

Now let's look for clues to help us make other people happy.

Perhaps you might help an old lady carry her shopping, or help a mother with her young children get out through the door of the shop. That would be good! Or give up your seat on the bus to an older person!

Perhaps you might smile at as many people as you can. That's easy! So is saying **"Thank you!"** And it spreads so much happiness!

And you now know what happens when you send out beautiful energy like this!

It's that boomerang again! That boomerang that is bringing happiness back to you in return for all the happiness you have just sent out to other people!

Cool!

So, now that I have given you some clues as to where to look for the clues, you have got to keep searching with your eyes all the time to see what is going on all around you, and to see what you can do to get more of those brownie points!

Keep looking! Keep listening!

Never give up! Never stop searching for clues!

Just keep thinking of all the brownie points you will gather up!

Well done!

BEING GRATEFUL!

You have so much to be grateful for!

Just think of all the good people and things in your life!

You have a wonderful body that does so much for you!

You can see with your eyes. You can hear with your ears. You can smell with your nose. You can taste with your mouth and tongue and you can feel by touching.

You can run, jump, laugh, cry, shout, whisper, hug.

You can read, count, do jig-saws, work out puzzles.

In return for all your body does for you, you must love your body. Instead of complaining that your nose is too long, the colour of your hair is wrong, you are too fat, too thin, too short, too tall, or whatever you do not like about your body, just stop for a minute and think!

Remember! You yourself chose the type of body you would have for this life-time! You chose what country you would live in, what nationality you would be, whether you would be rich or poor, what work you would do.

So, you chose your body for a particular reason! To learn some lesson!

You must respect, love and cherish your body! If you do not love yourself, how do you expect anyone else to love you?

Your body does not need to be made thinner or fatter, taller or shorter. You don't need to have a tattoo here or there. You are perfect as you are!

Remember again! You are made from God and God is perfect in every way! That means you too must be perfect!

And you are!

You must also be grateful for all the wonderful people you have in your life. Your parents, your friends, your brothers and sisters, your aunts and uncles, your grandparents.

Very often we take all these people for granted! We never tell them how much we love them or how grateful we are for all they do for us. You can change all that now by just saying **'Thank You'** to them! That will make them very happy!

There's a brownie point!

Think of all the other people who help you every day! The lollipop lady who guides you across the road safely. How often do you thank her? Thank her the next time she gets you across the road, smile at her, and watch as she smiles back at you! You have just spread a little bit of sunshine! You have just brightened up someone's day! How great is that!

The bus driver who drives you to school! Do you thank him as you get off the bus?

The dinner-ladies who make your dinner in school! Do you ever thank them?

All the people who serve you in the shops! Do you thank them?

The people who collect your rubbish! Do you thank them?

The people who clean the public toilets for us. What about them? Do you ever thank them?

The postman who brings all your letters and parcels to your door? Have you ever thanked him?

And why is it so important to thank everyone who helps us in some way?

Remember what I told you about the energy we send out?

Well, if we send out feelings of gratitude to everyone and to the universe, then what happens?

Remember the boomerang!

The universe sends us back more good things to be grateful for! How good is that!

It's like this. If you give a friend a gift, and they don't appreciate it, how does that make you feel? Will it make you feel you want to give them more gifts? I don't think so! But if they really are overjoyed to receive that gift,

how does that make you feel? Does it not make you feel
you want to give them more and more? Of course it does!
So, don't forget, the more gratitude you show for
everything you have in your life, the more good things will
come to you! That's the way it works!

What are you grateful for?

So instead of thinking about all the things you have not
got, think about all the things you have got. And be
grateful for everything! Even the rain! Especially the rain!
Everything has a reason and a purpose. And you know the
rain is necessary to make the crops, the grass, the
flowers and the trees all grow.

And you even enjoy the rain! Just put on your wellies and go out and have fun splashing about in the puddles. Listen to all the different musical notes the rain makes, with each little drop contributing a different sound, just like an orchestra, all playing together in perfect harmony.

Start to thank everyone you can for everything they do for you. Watch their faces light up with a smile! And just watch as lots more good things all find their way back to you in return.

It's Magic! Is it not?

FORGIVING

It can sometimes be very difficult to forgive those who hurt us or who are unkind to us.

But that is exactly what we must do! We must forgive!

Now remember how you learned early in this book that you can choose a lot of things to do with your life?

Well, you can also choose whether you forgive or whether you do not forgive.

Remember! You are in control!

But let's look at your options here!

Let's look at what happens when you choose to forgive, and at what happens if you choose not to forgive!

First, let's look at what happens if you choose not to forgive someone who has hurt you, or who has been nasty to you.

When you choose not to forgive, then you are holding a grudge, you are holding onto all those feelings of anger and bitterness.

And you remember learning about how your thoughts and feelings go out from you in the form of energy?

So here you are, sending out those ugly thoughts of anger and bitterness!

And you know what's going to happen!

It's that boomerang again! On its way back to you!

OUCH! That really hurt!

Of course it did! Because the thoughts and feelings you sent out attracted the same kind of stuff back to you!

So how could it not hurt?

And is there not enough of this ugly energy already out there without you adding to it?

Think about that one!

So choosing to not forgive is not really a good option, is it?

Now let's look at what happens when you choose to forgive!

When you choose to forgive, you are playing a very wise and clever game!

And why?

Because when you choose to forgive, you are actually helping yourself!

And how are you helping yourself?

You are helping yourself because you are ridding yourself of that burden of carrying around with you all that anger and bitterness. It is like taking an enormous weight off your shoulders! A huge weight that wears you down! A heavy chain around your neck!

All that hurting that has been hanging over you like a great black cloud!

And by choosing to forgive, you are releasing yourself from all that awful stuff!

You are freeing yourself from the hurt!

Yes! That's right!

You are actually freeing yourself from the hurt! You won't feel it any longer!

BE FREE

WOW! That wasn't hard!

And as an extra bonus, here's the boomerang again!

Only this time it's bringing a different type of energy back to you!

And this time, it definitely won't hurt!

So you now know what to do when someone hurts you. Instead of sending out feelings of anger towards them, change those feelings to feelings of love and forgiveness! And just see what happens!

Have you ever heard of *Mother Teresa*?

Mother Teresa spent her life helping the poor. And she

taught us some very important lessons.

One of the lessons Mother Teresa taught us was: *"Be kind to the kind and be kind to the unkind".*

You now know what this means!

Jesus, too, always taught about how important it is to forgive. Even as He was dying on the cross, He forgave all those who had crucified Him.

So now you know that holding onto grudges or bitter feelings does not do anyone any good whatsoever.

Now you know, that even though you still have a choice, the only sensible way to choose is to forgive.

That way, everyone's a winner!

Especially you!

ANGELS AND ARCHANGELS

Angels and Archangels are beings of very bright Light and are on a very high vibration level. Their auras are so bright that they shine out like wings behind them.

Remember what I told you about being close to God? How, when you are close to God, your aura is very bright, your energy is very strong, and you are on a very high vibration?

Let me explain this again!

When you are in a good mood and having an exciting, fun time, then how do you feel?

You feel on a high! You feel so excited! You have so much energy! You feel so good, you don't want this ever to stop! And you attract other people to you on the same energy level!

When you are not having so good a time, the opposite happens. You are feeling bored and you don't feel excited. Your energy is not just so high!

The difference in these two is that you are on a higher

vibration when you are happy. The happier you are and the more fun you are having, then the higher your energy is, and the higher the vibration you are on!

There are so many levels of vibration for your energy to be on!

The highest vibration of all is when you are really close to God.

And the angels are really close to God!

That's why their energy is so high, and because their energy is so high, they therefore vibrate at a very high rate.

The Light around all the angels is very bright. Sometimes they let us see them, but more often they let us feel them around us.

When you pray to the angels and ask them for help, they always answer you. But they can't help you unless you ask them to help. That's because you have free will, and the angels cannot help you until you freely choose to ask them.

And you can ask the angels to help in other parts of the world where people are suffering, where children are starving, where people are being killed. Once you ask, then flocks of angels go immediately to those places and help!

Isn't that magic? You and the angels can help the world in so many ways, but you have got to start everything by asking! You can send the angels wherever you think people are in trouble, and you know the angels will help!

Good for you!

Well done!

You and the angels!

What a team!

Archangels are very high mighty beings of Light. Probably the best known Archangels are Archangel Michael and Archangel Raphael, but there are many more. All of the

95

Archangels have a different colour.

Remember when you learned earlier in this book how to protect your energy from energy vampires?

Remember how you learned to draw the White Light around yourself?

Well, now that you have met Archangel Michael, there is a second way you can protect yourself.

Archangel Michael's colour is blue. Ask Archangel Michael to cover you with his blue cloak to protect you. He will always respond to you when you call on him. Sometimes, when you close your eyes at night just before you drift off to sleep, you might see a blue light. That's Archangel Michael coming to visit you and check that you are doing fine! Even during the day, whenever you sense a blue light around you, then you know Archangel Michael is with you, protecting you and looking after you. Isn't that just so cool?

Archangel Raphael is the Archangel who heals. Archangel Raphael's colour is a beautiful bright green. When Archangel Raphael puts his light around you, you will feel very peaceful and calm, and you will maybe actually see yourself being covered gently by his great big soft wings. How lovely is that!

Whenever you feel unwell, then if you ask Archangel Raphael to help you, he will!

You can call on Archangel Michael and Archangel Raphael any time you like, and they will always come to you. Don't forget to thank them!

As you grow older, you will learn about many more angels and Archangels.

But, of course, you have one very special angel all to yourself!

Your beautiful, magnificent, amazing Guardian Angel!

Let's now find out more about your own very special angel!

YOUR GUARDIAN ANGEL

From the minute you were born your Guardian Angel has been with you.

Your Guardian Angel is a special gift to you from God, to help you and to keep you safe.

Your Guardian Angel is a magnificent being of Light, and this magnificent being of Light is here just for you! Imagine! You have this great beautiful angel all to yourself! Awesome or what!

Your Guardian Angel knows all about you and sees everything. Your Guardian Angel sees all the kind deeds you do and that makes your Guardian Angel very happy.

And guess what! Your Guardian Angel also sees the not so good deeds you do, but loves you just the same!

Remember what I told you about what love means? It means accepting people exactly as they are! And that is exactly what your Guardian Angel does! Your Guardian Angel does not criticise you or complain to other angels about you. No! Your Guardian Angel sees you as the bright shining Light you really are! And your Guardian Angel is so happy to be your special angel! Your Guardian Angel is so proud of you! Always!

You must, of course, always ask your Guardian Angel for help! Remember what I told you about free will? Your

Guardian Angel cannot help you unless you ask for help and invite your angel in.

And remember what I told you about how you decide what lessons you want to learn in this life-time? How you created a plan for your life before you came here? When you were in Heaven and you decided, with the help of your friends, that you would like to live on Earth again?

Well, your Guardian Angel knows all about that plan that you created for yourself! And guess what! Your Guardian Angel is here to help you to stick to that plan and not get lost! But your Guardian Angel can't learn the lessons for you! Only you can do that! You can do that with the help of your Guardian Angel!

Talk to your Guardian Angel every day, and before you go off to sleep at night. Tell your Guardian Angel about how you feel, or if anything is worrying you. Your Guardian Angel will definitely make things right for you! Ask your Angel to

surround you and protect you with loving, soft, warm, angel wings! How lovely that feels!

How lucky we all are to have such a wonderful, magnificent being looking after us!

WOW!

WHO LOOKS AFTER THE FLOWERS AND TREES?

You now know that every living thing is made of energy. And you also know that every living thing is surrounded by an energy field called the *aura.*

You know too, that God has given you a special Guardian Angel to look after you and protect you, and help you to learn the lessons you have chosen to learn during your life-time.

And you know your Guardian Angel gives you unconditional love!

Well! Guess what!

Every other living thing has got someone looking after it as well!

See how God looks after all living things that God has created?

Every flower, every tree, and every little blade of grass each has a little Spirit helping them to grow.

We call these the *'little folk'* or the *'elementals'.*

And these elementals give unconditional love to their special charges! Just like the love you get from your very own Guardian Angel.

And you know how important love is!

Love is *soooooo* important that nothing in the garden can grow without it.

You have learned that God Intelligence is in every living thing. Remember?

Well, everywhere we look in Nature, there is an abundance of life. Some of this life we can see with our eyes, like the flowers, trees, mountains and rivers.

But some of this life we cannot see with our human eyes. And why is that?

Remember what you learned about energy and how all energy vibrates at different levels?

Well, all these little elementals are energy too, and they all vibrate at a higher level than we do. So that's why most of us cannot see them.

BUT! Some people can! That's because some people's energy vibration is on a higher level than most of the rest of us. And because of that, then the little fairies and pixies allow themselves to be seen by these people.

Perhaps you have seen some fairies in your garden?

Yes, fairies definitely do exist!

And what do these little elementals do all the time?

Well, they are looking after their special charges to help them grow.

And how do they do that?

They help the flowers and trees to grow by pouring some of their own energy into them.

That's why all the flowers are different colours!

All the little elementals have a different energy, and so each flower is a different colour, and each tree is a different shade of green!

How magical!

Have you ever hugged a tree?

Remember! A tree, like every other living thing, has an aura all around it. That's the tree's energy field. And when you hug a tree, that's what you will feel!

So go on! Give the next tree you pass a great big hug! The tree will love it! And so will you!

EXPERIMENT

Remember you learned how important love is? And how we all need love?

Well, now you know that all the trees and flowers need love too, in order to grow. And you know where they get love from! From all the little elementals looking after them!

Just to prove that love makes everything grow, try this experiment!

Ask your mum or dad to buy you a little seed of a flower that is not in season. Or maybe even a seed that has just started to grow.

Now, plant this little seed in a pot. Start to give this little seed love and as often as you can every day, talk to it kindly, tell it how you love it so much and how you want it to grow.

Remember to give it some water, of course! It needs water as well as lots of love.

Watch what happens!

OTHER NATURE HELPERS

It is not just the flowers and trees that are looked after by little Spirit helpers.

So too, the rivers, the streams, the oceans and the mountains all have a protector who looks after them.

The little water Spirits who look after the rivers and streams are called *'undines'*, *'sprites'* and *'sylphs'*.

Sometimes, when you stand quietly beside a gushing stream and listen very carefully, you might just hear the laughter and squeals of these little water Spirits, as they tumble down over the rocks and stones, racing each other in the flow of the water. You might even see them as little bright, sparkling lights as they flash past you.

That is just the water sprites, the undines and the sylphs having fun!

Other elementals look a bit like *Tinkerbell,* with transparent wings and energy shapes that look like bodies and which change colour all the time.

There are also fairies who work with fire.

Have you ever sat and gazed into a fire? Perhaps into a bonfire? Or perhaps the fire in your sitting room? Or even the flame of a candle?

What did you see there?

Shapes? Colours? Images?

These are called the *'salamanders'*, and they are very powerful and very magical.

Very young children can stare for a long time into the fire. Why?

Remember what you read about babies arriving into this world from the much higher energy vibration level of Heaven? Remember you learned why they sleep a lot?

Well, for the first five or six years of your life, you are still very close to that high vibration level, as your soul gets used to being on the much lower, Earth energy vibration level.

So you are still *'in tune'* with Heaven, and that is why you might very well be able to see all these little elementals, sprites, undines and salamanders.

Perhaps you see them a lot, and you haven't told anyone because you think you are just imagining things?

Well, believe me! You are not imagining things! Far from it!

All of these really do exist!

And here is something even more amazing!

Unicorns and dragons exist too!

All of these exist on a higher energy vibration level than humans do. You now know what that means! And you understand why most people cannot see them! Simply because their energy vibration is not high enough!

But you might be able to see them!

Lucky, lucky, you!

EXPERIMENT - HOW TO CHOOSE YOUR CRYSTAL!

Crystals, stones and gems are all very beautiful!

But do you know where they come from?

They come from deep down inside the Earth.

And because they come from deep inside the Earth, they are a form of life.

And because they are a form of life, they send out energy.

Remember how you learned that the energy you send out through your aura attracts the same kind of energy back to you?

And how that is the same with all energy?

Well, the energy the crystal or the stone sends out does exactly the same!

So, when you are in a shop choosing a crystal, how do you know which crystal to choose?

Well, believe it or not, you don't choose the crystal! In actual fact, the crystal chooses you!

How come?

Let me explain!

When you are in the shop, looking around at all the beautiful crystals, rocks and stones, they all sense your energy. And there will be one particular crystal or stone that will really like your energy, because it is very similar to its own energy.

So what do you do? You let your hand hover over all the stones and crystals, and whenever you feel a very gentle pull, then that's your crystal calling to you! That particular crystal's energy will pull on your energy!

It's like the crystal is saying to you, **"Over here! Hello! Please take me home!"**

So you see, you can never choose the wrong crystal!

And you know why!

Because the crystal chooses you!

WOW! More magic!

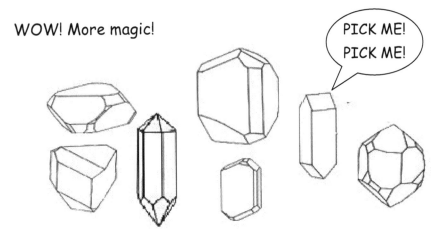

THE MAGIC OF SPRING

Spring is the time of year when Nature awakens from its long winter sleep.

Just as you get up every morning fresh from your sleep, so too Nature is now returning to life.

And what beautiful life we see all around us!

The trees are beginning to bud and flowers are beginning to peep out above the ground.

The birds are beginning to build their nests.

The days are growing longer and warmer.

Perhaps you felt that your garden, or the park in your town, was missing something over the winter months? Well, you were right! All of Nature's energy was underground, resting.

Now it is spring, and Mother Nature is returning, so you can feel the energy returning to your garden, to the woods and to the parks.

Remember what you learned in the last chapter about how all the flowers and trees are looked after by all the little Nature helpers?

Well, now it is spring again, and the daffodils, the primroses, the bluebells and all the different flowers are being helped to grow by the little fairies and elemental spirits looking after them and breathing life into them. Remember! That's how all the flowers have different colours! Each little fairy or Nature Spirit is different, and so when they all breathe their essence into the flowers, a different colour comes into each flower!

Magic! The magic of spring!

Spring brings us all new life and energy. We all feel as if we too, have been sleeping for a long time and we are now ready to jump back into life again!

THE MAGIC OF SUMMER

Everyone loves summer!

Nature is so beautiful in summer!

There is so much magic all around us!

All the bright colours of the flowers and trees!

And you now know how they all got their different colours!

You now know all about the magic and how it works!

All the little fairies and Nature spirits are so happy because they have all done their work to perfection! Their flowers have all bloomed and they are spreading so much happiness to everyone.

Summer gives us all an opportunity to connect with Mother Nature much more easily.

When you walk in your bare feet in the grass, then you can feel the earth's energy very strongly. When you lie down in the grass and close your eyes and then let your hands touch the ground, you are really connecting with Mother Earth!

Mother Earth just loves your gentle touch! It's like you giving a hug to someone! Mother Nature just loves your hugs!

The little streams gurgle over the stones as they wind their way along. The little water spirits, the little undines and sprites are so happy! They laugh and giggle as they tumble down the water, really having a fun time! If you listen very carefully, you might feel their energy as they go past you!

Magic!

Everyone feels good in summer. That's because Nature is giving us so much energy!

See how Nature shares everything with us and helps us feel good?

THE MAGIC OF AUTUMN

Nature's beautiful autumn coat of many colours!

Autumn is such a colourful season!

This is Nature dazzling us with her beauty before she retires for her long winter sleep.

So many colours!

Cherry reds, flaming reds, dark reds, yellows, coppers, golds, browns, orange, green, all sparkling when the sun shines on them!

So much magic all around us! Those Nature helpers have been really busy!

How gently the multi-coloured leaves fall to earth when the time is right for the trees to let them go!

The woods and forests are magnificent in autumn!

There is a carpet of all colours for you to walk on!

Autumn is the time of harvesting too. The crops are fully grown and the fruit trees are over-loaded with all the different kinds of delicious fruits.

And you know how all that fruit got there! It's those Nature helpers again!

All that fruit just ready for picking! And, of course, for eating!

Mother Nature just gives us so much!

THE MAGIC OF WINTER

Winter creates such a magical fairy world!

The frost sparkles and glitters, like little tiny gems all lighting up at the same time.

The snow glistens and glows under the light of the moon at night and under the light of the sun during the day.

This is the season when Nature wears her winter coat of white.

When Nature puts on her winter coat, everything looks like a great big wedding cake covered in icing.

It is so pretty! So full of magic!

The tiny snowflakes flutter down to earth, meandering here and there as they descend. Each one is different. The little water sprite in each flake is happy to be alive, floating downwards  with all the others. What fun they are all having! Chasing each other and tumbling down, over and across each other!

Little tiny jewels of frozen water plummeting to earth, in a free-falling somersault. Little tiny jewels that cling onto everything for dear life. They hang from the clothes line, from the branches of the trees, from the fences. And what fun you can have when you shake the clothes line and watch them tumble right down to the ground to join all the others!

This is Mother Nature putting on a grand show just for you!

Then, when they pile up in a soft carpet on the ground they make everywhere look just so magical! As if someone has taken a great big paint brush and painted everything white.

Nature glows, it sparkles, it shimmers, it shines when the ground is covered with snow and frost.

That's when the fun really begins!

That's when we make snowballs and snowmen.

Your snowman stands so proudly in your garden! Then when the moon comes out, the magic really starts! Everything lights up in the magical light of the moon! Some trees do not go to sleep during the winter months. These are what we call *deciduous* trees. They do not shed their leaves like the other trees, so their little Nature helpers are still with them in winter. What a really fun time these little Nature spirits have sliding down the moon beams and playing in the magic of the moon light!

Everything is very quiet when the snow is on the ground. A kind of hush hangs over everything.

All the little insects and animals are hidden underground.

Mother Nature is looking after them there, keeping them warm and cosy!

All the little fairies and Nature Spirits are underground too, having a long rest. Their little charges, the flowers, are having a rest too, so there is not much for them to do right now. So they are just taking it easy!

Lots of animals go to sleep for the whole of winter. We call this their 'Hibernation'. A long sleep means that they will have lots of energy when spring comes, when they will wake up again.

See how Nature takes care of everything!

And, of course, Nature takes care of you too!

COME TO THE PARTY!

What a lot you have learned in this book!

How much more knowledge you now have than before!

You have learned about the real you, about where you have come from and why you are here.

You also know a lot more about God.

And you now know about energy and how energy works.

So, think of life as a great big party!

A great fun game that you are here to play!

And, as in every game, there are some rules.

You know what the rules in the game of life are!

Think of the boomerang!

Think of the brownie points!

Think of finding the hidden clues!

It's always very important to have knowledge. But it is even more important to use that knowledge in the correct way!

So what are you going to do with all the knowledge you

now have?

You are going to do what you came here to Planet Earth to do!

You are going to spread love!

And you are going to have fun!

You don't go to a party to hide behind the door. No, you go to a party to enjoy yourself, to have fun and to mix with other people.

It's the same with life!

You came here to spread love and to learn a lot of lessons, and at the same time to have fun while you are doing all that!

And if you stick to the rules and play by the rules, which

you now know, then your life will be full of magic, fun, laughter and, of course, love!

And you can't ask for any better than that!

So have a wonderful life, remembering what you have learned!

Remember that you are not just a physical body! You are a soul as well!

Remember that we are all One in the great God Energy!

And remember that because we are all One, we must treat each other kindly. We must share, we must forgive, and we must show we are grateful for absolutely everything that we have, and for everything that happens to us.

And, of course, remember the boomerang!

Remember that the boomerang always brings back to you what you send out!

So laugh a lot, love a lot and make other people happy.

And then you will be happy too!

FUN ACTIVITIES!

Now for some fun activities for you all to try!

These will help you to keep the positivity flowing in your life!

And then you will feel good!

A HAPPY JAR

At home, we all throw jam jars out every day. Now, instead of throwing them out, you can take one of these jars, clean it out and make it your own.

You can decorate the jar whatever way you want. You can write out lots of happy, positive thoughts and put them all in the jar. Now, whenever you are feeling sad, lonely, angry or worried, then all you have to do is go to your jar and take out some happy thoughts. When you do this you will see how quickly your mood will change to one of happiness!

Cool or what?

In your *Happy Jar* you can also put in

any items that bring back good memories. For example a pebble you may have picked up on the beach when you were there with your family, or a feather you may have found when you were out for a walk with your friends.

Put your special jar in a place where you can see it, and above all, enjoy and treasure it!

Your special jar will keep you happy!

You really will have *happiness in a jar*!

INSPIRATION JOURNAL

An *Inspiration Journal* is a very special notebook that you can make into something that will help you see how truly amazing and unique you really are!

Remember earlier in this book where you learned how important it is to be grateful for everything and every person you have in your life?

Well, when you give thanks for everything in your life, you are showing gratitude.

Examples of *gratitudes* are:

- **THANK YOU FOR MY LIFE**

- **THANK YOU FOR MY FAMILY**

- **THANK YOU FOR NATURE**

- **THANK YOU FOR MY HOME**

- **THANK YOU FOR MY FRIENDS, ETC.**

You are now going to think up as many gratitudes as you can, and write them all into your journal!

Think about it this way!

When we receive a present from someone, we always say

'*Thank You!*'

But remember! God has given us the greatest gift of all, which is the gift of *LIFE,* and all the lovely things that come with it! So we should really be very thankful every day for all of this!

The next things to enter in your journal are your *I AM affirmations.*

An affirmation is simply saying words of encouragement, and in this case these words are about yourself. Examples of I AM affirmations are:

- **I AM HAPPY**

- **I AM POSITIVE**

- **I AM GRATEFUL**

- **I AM STRONG**

- **I AM THE BEST PRSON THAT I CAN BE, etc.**

What you put in your journal is totally up to you. You could draw some pictures of your family, slot some photographs in, or write something really nice about yourself. Then, in turn, if there comes a time when you are not feeling positive for some reason, just look back in your journal and remind yourself of how amazing you really are! And of all the good things you have in your life!

That will change your unhappy mood!

What are you grateful for?

_____

_____

_____

_____

PILLOWCASE OF POSITIVITY

For this activity you will need a white pillowcase and some different colours of fabric pens.

On your pillowcase, write down positive words about yourself. You can also sketch things on it that make you happy. Draw a picture of what you would like to do for a living when you get older, or a picture showing your favourite hobby.

Friendly   **Loved**

Unique

Happy

wonderful

Special

caring

Nice

Good

Joyful

The important thing to remember, is that this pillowcase is your creation, and what you put on it is entirely up to you. So be as creative and colourful as you can!

Once finished, your pillowcase can be put on your bed. Imagine going to bed every night and laying your head down on all your positive thoughts and dreams for the future!!!!!

How good does that feel?

VISION BOARD

A *Vision Board* is a really fun activity to do and it is basically a large picture, with all the things that make you happy in your life at present, and your aims and goals for the future.

You will need a large sheet of coloured paper, lots of magazines, coloured markers, scissors and glue.

First, go through all your magazines and cut out all the pictures you like, especially pictures that show you what you would like to be in the future. Cut out too, pictures of all the things that you have in your life right now that make you happy. If you would really like a dog, for example, you could cut out a picture of a cute, cuddly little puppy.

Once you have cut out all your pictures, stick them on your Vision Board and decorate it with positive words and lots of colour.

The key to this activity is to put your Vision Board in a place where you can see it every day. Then it will remind you of your aims and goals! A good place to put it might be on your bedroom wall, or on your playroom wall.

Don't forget to clean up after you have finished!

BUBBLEWRAP

I am sure you have all seen bubblewrap. I am sure too that you all just love squeezing and bursting all those bubbles!

Bursting bubblewrap, however, is not just fun!

Bursting bubblewrap is a really good activity to do if you are feeling stressed, anxious or angry.

Let me explain!

Cut a length of bubblewrap and place it on the ground in front of you. Now take a deep breath and stomp all over it, making sure that you burst all the bubbles.

Don't miss any!

As you stomp all over the bubbles, really feel as if you are letting out all your anger and getting rid of all the issues that you are finding hard to deal with.

By doing this simple activity, what is actually happening?

You are sending all your negative energy down into Mother Earth and Mother Earth will dispose of it for you.

Remember earlier you learned about how kind Mother Earth is, and all the good things Mother Earth does for each one of us?

Well, here is another way in which Mother Earth helps us!

You will definitely feel much better after stomping over all those bubbles!

BALL OF POSITIVITY

This is a great activity when you join with some others of your own age!

Get a ball, and begin to pass it to each other. As each of you catches the ball in turn, you have to shout out something good about yourself!

If someone cannot think of anything good to shout out, then you can shout out for them!

But remember! It must be something *good*!

HAPPINESS CARD

Make a small card and on it write a big heading saying that the person who has this card must do a good deed for someone.

This good deed could be something as small as smiling at someone in town, or helping your mum with the dishes or housework. Once you have done a good deed for someone, then pass the card over to them, and ask them, in turn, to now do a good deed for someone else.

Then they will pass the card on further.

See what you have started?

You have created a chain of happiness!

You have started a little ripple that will grow into a tsunami!

See the power you have?

The power to spread happiness!

WOW!

Now that we have come to the end of 'RAINBOWS, ANGELS and UNICORNS', and before we say 'Bye' to Mattie and Maggie, here are 3 special drawings for you to colour in!

First, the RAINBOW!

There are 7 colours in the rainbow. Do you remember what they are?

These colours are: red, orange, yellow, green, blue, indigo and violet.

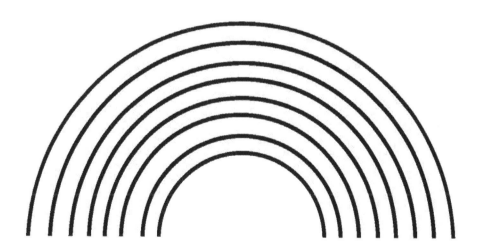

The second drawing is of an angel. Remember you read about how angels come in all different colours?

So what colours are you going to use for this magnificent angel?

This final picture is of a Unicorn in a forest, with lots of bluebells. When the bluebells bloom, that is a clear sign that spring has arrived, and that means Nature is alive again!

Even though these flowers are called bluebells, they are really more violet or light purple in colour. Can you see them in the picture? And the Unicorn? Now you can colour them all in!

Eileen McCourt

BYE!

Eileen McCourt

Printed in Great Britain
by Amazon

33688112R00090